MW01526743

Remark
9/11 and

"The [2,200] architects and engineers that I represent have found evidence that has not been told to the American people by the agencies tasked with explaining the destruction of these towers—evidence of *controlled demolition*, particularly with the third high-rise that collapsed on that day in the afternoon of 9/11, World Trade Center 7... Here is a 47-storey skyscraper, at 5:20 in the afternoon, it drops like a rock and I mean this fast (*demonstrating with pen dropping*), free-fall acceleration, straight down, uniformly, symmetrically, as you saw. Now a building with 40,000 tons of structural steel cannot fall straight-down, like we saw, due to normal office fires, the official reason given us by NIST (National Institute of Standards and Technology) without all 80 columns on each floor being removed simultaneously, and then synchronistically-timed floor-by-floor... Normal office fires have never brought down a skyscraper ever before."— RICHARD GAGE, Architect, Member of the American Institute of Architects, Founder of Architects & Engineers for 9/11 Truth (AE911 Truth)

"The World Trade 7 Building reminds me of the Meridian Bank Building in some ways, in Philadelphia. The Meridian Bank Building is a 38-storey skyscraper that burned for 18 hours in 1991, suffered extensive damage from the fire, but did not collapse."—JOEL MILLER, High-Rise Architect

"There has never been, till 9/11, an experience where a high-rise building that was steel-framed completely collapsed. There have been fires that have burned longer in similar structures without any collapse."—SCOTT GRAINGER, P.E., Forensic Fire Protection Engineer

"It's just like taking your car keys out and just dropping them. That's how fast the building [WTC7] came down, for over 100 feet, and the only way you can get that is when there is 'zero resistance' and so what we're looking at is a building just coming straight down, falling right through itself with zero resistance. Buildings don't have zero resistance, which is why you feel comfortable just walking into a building."—DAVID CHANDLER, M.S., B.S. Physics, M.S. Mathematics

"Building 7 came down—it went into a sudden collapse across the full width to the left of the building for 2.25 seconds, which amounted to 105 feet, or eight 13-foot-tall stories. It was a full free-fall acceleration. That is impossible because in a natural collapse columns would have to buckle. When columns buckle there is a minimum resistance—it's isotonic, you know what that means, it means it never goes to zero—so it's impossible."—TONY SZAMBOTI, B.S.M.E. Mechanical Engineer

"The most obvious would be the fact that these two buildings, which were steel-framed high-rise buildings, and when we're talking about steel-framed the point is that there were 287 steel columns that went from the sub-basements through the roof and the lower floors these were absolutely massive, they taper off of course as you go to the top. The ones in the—and I'm talking here about the core columns—there were 47 core columns and then 240 columns around the outside. For the building to come down as they did, straight down, all 287 steel columns had to fail *simultaneously*. Think about that. And the theory is that it was fire that caused the steel columns to weaken and that's what brought the building down. Well, first of all, steel-framed high-rise buildings have never come down because of fire."—DAVID RAY GRIFFIN, retired Professor of Theology, author of *The New Pearl Harbor: Disturbing Questions about the Bush Administration and 9/11*

"There is a technology that exists that can do this. That technology can also be used for free energy... There exists a technology where instead of molecules being attracted to each other, they repel each other. What happened is not impossible because it happened."—DR. JUDY WOOD, former Professor of Mechanical Engineering, author of *Where Did the Towers Go? Evidence of Directed Free-energy Technology on 9/11*

Select books by PARIS TOSEN

NON-FICTION

Reality Science
The Book of Stelans
God is DNA
American Androids Critical Edition
The Polymerase Fantasy

FICTION

Master of the Androids
The Satellite People
Sesame Century

500 TRILLION TO ONE

Odds of Collapsing Three Towers

PARIS TOSEN

CANADA

This is a work of non-fiction.

First edition, March 2014
Second edition, May 2015

ISBN 978-1-496191-04-5 (ppk)
ISBN 978-1-926949-64-2 (eBook)

www.tosen.ca

CONTENTS

1. INTRODUCTION

On September 11, 2001, 19 Islamic terrorists hijacked four passenger jets and attacked several targets in the United States including New York City. The total death toll was estimated at about 3,000 people.

That Tuesday morning in New York, two Boeing 767s, American Airlines Flight 11 and United Airlines Flight 175, struck the 110-floor Twin Towers of the World Trade Center (WTC 1 and WTC 2). By 10:28 am both buildings had collapsed into their own footprint as a direct result of fire-induced structural failure. Debris from the North Tower fell onto 47-floor WTC 7 and caused extensive fire and structural damage, WTC 7 also collapsed perfectly into its own footprint at 5:21 pm.

The collapse of these three steel-framed buildings, despite the official statements from the 9/11 Commission and other experts, presented a real mystery because at no time in the history of steel-framed buildings had they ever collapsed under any reason, according to architects and engineers. Given no evidence of a steel-framed building ever collapsing due to fire, I decided to apply probability to the 9/11 mystery.

But what I wanted to do was to put aside all the arguments, including the views of conspiracy theorists. I needed the best environment for my mathematical applications, and because I wasn't a mathematician I wanted to apply basic formulas so that others could understand what I was doing. It would have defeated my purpose to hire some advanced mathematician to invent a logarithm to explain the probability of three buildings collapsing perfectly due to the crash of two airliners. In order to work from the cleanest slate possible I opted for my own probability guesswork thinking that anyone could follow. The democratization of knowledge seemed reasonable and would avoid the pitfalls of any complicated theory. But I was biased in my view that the events of 9/11 were not adequately explained by the NIST (National Institute of Standards and Technology) investigations, completed in 2005 and 2008.

The situation was very straightforward in my view: on that fateful day two planes hit two towers and three towers collapsed and they collapsed perfectly into their own footprint. What was the probability of that series of events?

The only way to see through the overwhelming fallout was to simplify the investigation. If we were to strip away all the excesses from 9/11–the burning towers, the thousands of deaths, the destruction, the terrorist groups, the security breaches, the government rhetoric, the tragedy, the pulverized concrete, the fires, the dust and the sounds–we would eventually find ourselves looking at two hijacked airliners headed towards the city of New York on the fateful morning of September 11, 2001. This is what happened:

(a)
Plane #1 hit **NORTH** TOWER
American Airlines **Flight 11**

(b)
Plane #2 hit **SOUTH** TOWER
United Airlines **Flight 175**

I don't want to diminish the significance of the event but I do want to remove the noise so we can study the crime scene.

As far as *probability* is concerned, we wouldn't need to know if these planes, two of four (also, Flight 77 and Flight 93) that were hijacked that morning, were taken by a group of terrorists or if they were inserted by a team of secret commandos or if even they were remotely-controlled. Those are details we can argue later on.

By putting many of the nonessential details aside, we get to focus on the fundamentals. The fundamentals allow us a chance to learn some key insights into this kind of event. We can then rely on these insights later on as more and more details cloud the issue.

I want to find out the probability of these two planes directly hitting each of the 110-story Twin Towers at the World Trade Center. I want to find out the probability of those Twin Towers collapsing perfectly into their own footprint. And I want to include the probability of Tower 7 collapsing perfectly into its own footprint as well. So I need three sets of data:

1. The probability of the two planes each hitting one of the Twin Towers.

2. The probability of the three towers collapsing due to fire.

3. The probability of the three towers collapsing perfectly into their own footprint.

These three data sets are *interrelated* and if one set doesn't work then it will ripple into the other sets. For example, if only one of those planes hit the tower, the deal is off. The official story wouldn't work. Had only one tower fallen then that too would not have had the same effect; less people would have died, less devastation, and perhaps the third tower wouldn't have fallen either. The *trigger* of the two initial collapsed towers was the two planes and the *trigger* for the third tower collapse was the two towers. All of them are inextricably intertwined. In other words, we need **all three outcomes** in order to replicate the sequence of events that happened on September 11. And, mathematically speaking, we have to replicate those key events since that is what has been recorded in the history books. The math won't lie. *If those events defy the math then something is wrong with the official 9/11 story.* From this data we can derive the probability of the entire sequence of events.

Each plane was piloted by an amateur pilot flying a modern commercial airliner traveling at over 500 mph. The planes weighed in excess of 300,000 lbs loaded with passengers (American 11, 87 passengers; United 175, 60 passengers) plus 5 hijackers in each. The planes were not advanced fighter jets. These were wide-bodied aircraft. They did not have the manoeuvrability of fighter jets. These commercial jets were traveling at about 750 feet per second so decisions counted and so did degrees of accuracy.

There wasn't much chance to make a wrong decision and having never taken this action, having never hijacked a Boeing 767 with the intent to crash it into an iconic tower structure we can infer that these two pilots were dead focused on their task at hand. Any error on their part as they approached the Twin Towers could cause delay, or worse, failure of their suicide mission.

2. ASSUMPTIONS

Inevitably we have to figure out the probability of them hitting their marks. The two outcomes that we all witnessed on that day—two planes each hitting squarely one of the Twin Towers—are really two outcomes of many outcomes. For some reason these outcomes have been grossly overlooked. But before we run through the outcomes, let us present a set of assumptions. Here are my four assumptions:

1. **Each outcome is equally likely.** The outcomes that occurred were two of many that could have occurred, each of them equally likely to occur. In other words, the outcomes that we saw were not set in stone. This is fundamental to my probability analysis.

2. **Both pilots were skilled.** We will give the hijackers the "benefit of the doubt" and assume they had enough skill to accomplish their tasks, for whatever reason. The investigation into 9/11

uncovered the fact that the hijackers took some courses at a flight school. It was never uncovered that they were trained to pilot wide-bodied jet airliners. For the purpose of our discussion, we will say that an average veteran pilot has 20 years' worth of flight experience and hours, and then we will say that these rogue pilots somehow managed to accumulate 2 years' worth of flight experience. This would give them enough ability to pilot the crafts but then also separates them from true veterans. The ratio here is 10:1, or 10%. But a person with zero experience could not adequately manoeuvre the planes and therefore could never accomplish the task. They had enough skill to attempt the flight tasks and for one reason or another they were successful.

3. **No prior rehearsal.** The airline hijackers were doing this for the first time. It could be later argued that the pilots were involved in some secretive flight training exercises. In any case we will take the position that these pilots were attempting this for the first time.

4. **Plane crashes are independent.** Whether the first plane hits or misses it doesn't affect the hit or miss of the second plane, and vice versa.

Had the first plane missed, we don't know if it would have first circled around before the second plane hit. Plane #1 could have missed and that would have meant Plane #2 hitting first. We assume they would have kept trying to hit unless they crashed, were shot down, or ran out of fuel. Ironically, our job is made easier because of the fact that both planes hit as planned. Again, we do not need the reason of their precision for this probability analysis.

3. STEEL-FRAMED BUILDINGS DOWN

"No steel-framed high rise building has ever collapsed due to fire, and we have over 100 examples from which to choose," said architect Richard Gage, founder of *Architects & Engineers for 9/11 Truth* and a member of the *American Institute of Architects*. His view echoes that of theologian and author of *The New Pearl Harbor* David Ray Griffin, another member of the 9/11 Truth Movement.

Steel-framed buildings have never collapsed in the history of the world. That all changed on September 11, 2001 when three steel-framed buildings completely collapsed. All of them due to fire-induced damage. The official explanation for the Twin Towers and World Trade Center Building 7 collapsing was due to extensive fire and structural damage.

Since the only time in history, not one but three steel-framed buildings collapsed was on 9/11, I wanted to determine the odds of this rare event happening because whatever happened, it beat the odds. It was an unprecedented historical event. The attacks on 9/11 changed America forever. This led to a protracted 12-year conflict (Iraq War officially ended December 31, 2011) in Afghanistan and Iraq that according to former chief economist Joseph Stiglitz has cost the United States over $3 trillion, far greater than the $60 billion estimate from the Bush administration.

3.1 Getting the details

The towers were struck by the planes in this order

Plane #1 — WTC 1 — 8:46 am

Plane #2 — WTC 2 — 9:03 am

3.2 A little more background

Then-president George W. Bush in his speech said, "The terrorist attacks can shake the foundations of our biggest buildings but they cannot touch the foundation of America. These acts shattered steel, but they cannot dent the steel of American resolve. America was targeted for attack because we're the brightest beacon for freedom and opportunity in the world." In his 2002 State of the Union speech President Bush reiterated his tone on the subject of the 9/11 events: "On September the Eleventh, enemies of freedom committed an act of war against our country. Americans have known wars, but for the past 136 years they have been wars on foreign soil except for one Sunday in 1941. Americans have known the casualties of war, but not at the center of a great city on a peaceful morning. Americans have known surprise attacks but never before on thousands of civilians. All of this was brought upon us in a single day, and night fell on a different world. A world where freedom itself is under attack."

Barack Obama would not take office until 2008, seven years after the attacks, but the views of the White House hadn't changed. "There are still some who would question, or even justify the offenses of 9/11, but let us be clear, al'Qaeda killed nearly 3,000 people on that day. The victims were innocent men, women and children from America and many other nations who had done nothing to anybody," said President Obama.

On that day, three steel-framed buildings collapsed. They set a new precedent for never in history did fire collapse a building. Mechanical Engineer Tony Szamboti, an engineer with over

20 years of experience in the aerospace industry, is certain of this fact: "To reinforce this point, we hear often that no steel-frame building has ever collapsed due to fire. In reality, it's even stronger than that—no steel-frame building, super-structure type building, has ever collapsed [itself to the ground], not for any reason—any reason— hurricanes, tornadoes, fires, airplane hits... any reason other than controlled demolition. I'm not talking about a warehouse with a single roof which is basically one beam. I'm talking about a superstructure where it's a grid stacked one on top of the other. That has never happened. No building with that type of construction has ever collapsed, in the history of the world."

Szamboti started researching into the 9/11 events in 2006 after reading a paper by Dr. Steven Jones, an American physics professor at Brigham Young University, and his description of "huge amounts of molten metal" found in the three collapsed buildings in New York. In late 2005, Jones questioned the mainstream collapse theory of the World Trade Center towers and WTC 7 and suggested in a research paper, *Why Indeed Did the WTC Buildings Collapse?* that the buildings collapsed due to controlled demolition, possibly because of nanothermite applications, atomic-scaled reactant particles that can store and release more energy than any conventional explosives. A year later, Jones was placed on paid leave and subsequently retired.

There are many who questioned the official story, far too many to discuss here, but they also include people like Dr. Steve Pieczenik, a former Deputy Assistant Secretary of State under three different US Administrations and an expert in psychological operations, who was told by a top general that 9/11 was a false flag operation and that Osama bin Laden died in 2001 after having been treated by CIA physicians. (CIA Analyst Jack Ryan from Tom Clancy's novels is loosely based on Pieczenik.)

3.3 The collapse of the towers

The towers collapsed in this order

(a) WTC 2 — 9:59 am

(b) WTC 1 — 10:28 am

WTC 2 (South Tower) burned for 56-minutes before collapsing. WTC 1 (North Tower) burned for 102-minutes before collapsing. Note that the tower that was struck second fell first and we

have no real explanation for why the north tower
needed another 29-minutes to collapse.

The official explanation of both collapses would
be due to fire damage as a result of burning fuel
and damaged thermal insulation (ie fireproofing
was blown off). It bears worth repeating that the
details of that terrible day are put aside in order
to arrive at the probability figures. As such I am
relying on the official statements on 9/11 and not
taking into account any conspiracy theory in
regards to this particular discussion.

3.4 The probability of collapsing WTC2

What then is the probability of the South Tower
(WTC 2) collapsing due to fire?

If we use a conservative figure—say we borrow
Gage's observation

> "no steel-framed high rise has ever collapsed
> due to fire in over **100 cases**"

It is far below the real figure, but 100 will work
for our purposes. We can say that the chance of
the South Tower collapsing is

1 in 100 (1%)

We have a fair and reasonable approximation of the first collapse. It's never happened before. We could use a larger figure like 1,000 but I have decided from the start to be generous with my assumptions and to be conservative in my calculations.

The mathematical expression is:

0.01 (1%)

Some say that the South Tower was collapsed due to planted demolitions, including the use of nanothermite explosives. Gage is well aware of this possibility and has good reasons for it. "Had they acknowledged it, they would have had to acknowledge that fires alone are only 1,500 to 1,700 degrees—cannot possibly have created several tons of molten iron. Doesn't happen. But what can—thermite. Thermite creates molten iron as its by-product and we have the chemical evidence of thermite in the dust, in the molten iron, and in the slag at the ends of..." Gage said during a street-based activism.

Gage differs with the research of former professor of mechanical engineering, Dr. Judy Wood, who thinks that the presence of *tritium* (a rare radioactive isotope) without the ionization is suggestive of a cold fusion-type weapon.

I say we continue to accept the official statements for the time being in order to calculate our figures properly. If we were to admit the use of demolitions or exotic weapons then that would change all our assumptions and we'd have to start again. Plus, there's never been any evidence to substantiate the claim that any of the towers were demolished.

3.5 The probability of collapsing WTC1

Not only did the South Tower go, but at 10:28 am the North Tower collapsed after 102-minutes of burning.

What is the probability of the North Tower collapsing due to fire alone?

1 in 100 (1%)

If in over 100 cases no fire has ever brought down this type of building then we can generously say that it happens roughly 1-percent of the time, given the fact that the trend shifted on September 11. The odds of the North Tower falling are 100:1, the same as the South Tower.

3.6 The probability of collapsing WTC7

In the previous sections we found the probability of towers 1 and 2 collapsing due to fire. The third tower that was on fire that day was not hit by an airplane. Officially, WTC 7 was hit by falling debris from the North Tower. The North Tower was situated about a football field away. The official report said that the falling debris created the fires in Tower 7. It wasn't as hot as the first two towers and it burned for nearly 7 hours.

(c) WTC 7 — 5:21 pm

The collapse of Tower 7 is a hot issue in the conspiracy theory debate. Many people believe, having examined and discussed the evidence that Tower 7 did not collapse due to fire, rather it was brought down specifically by controlled demolitions.

When Danny Jowenko, a Dutch demolitions expert, was shown the collapse of WTC 7 in a taped interview, without knowing it was WTC 7, he immediately commented, (translation) "That is controlled demolition." Then he added: "It's been imploded. It's a hired job, done by a team of experts." Jowenko later died when he crashed his car into a tree.

What is the probability of Tower 7, a steel-framed building, collapsing due to fire?

1 in 100 (1%)

The probability is the same as the South Tower and North Tower. The probability is 1-percent. Independently, each of these World Trade Center towers has a 1% chance of collapsing due to fire. We haven't accounted for the perfect fall into each of their respective footprints yet. We are just saying that the odds of each building collapsing was 100 to 1. We're not finished yet because, as it turned out, all three towers fell on the same day and we have to account for that in our math.

4. POSSIBLE OUTCOMES

The events of 9/11 were remarkable because they represented a coordinated attack on the United States. They were attributed directly to the global terrorist organization al'Qaeda, a militant Islamist group masterminded, dead or alive, by Osama bin Laden.

Early that morning, these two Boeing 767 airliners flown by pilots just out of flight school rammed into each of the Twin Towers. It had never been attempted before. Crashing a plane into a tower was an impressive feat, especially for an untrained pilot under extreme stress and in enemy air space.

4.1 The probability of a direct hit on a skyscraper

We have to take into account the triggers for the tower collapses and there are two that we know of—two Boeing 767s. We will now look at the probability of a direct hit on a skyscraper by an airplane. Before we can calculate the probability we first have to go over the possible outcomes since the number of outcomes will be the basis for our calculation.

4.2 Extracurricular possible outcomes

The outcomes that could have happened, but for whatever reason did not occur, still have to be accounted for in our probability analysis. There are 11 extracurricular outcomes for this event:

1. Plane #1 could have been shot down by US Air Force jets.

2. Plane #2 could have been shot down by US Air Force jets.

3. Due to the almost surgical nature of the attacks, the jet engines of Plane #1 could have failed and the plane would have prematurely crashed.

4. Due to the almost surgical nature of the attacks, the jet engines of Plane #2 could have failed and the plane would have prematurely crashed.

5. Due to pilot inexperience, Pilot #1 may have lost control during their final approach and the planes could have prematurely crashed.

21

6. Due to pilot inexperience, Pilot #2 may have lost control during their final approach and the planes could have prematurely crashed.

7. Plane #1 may have veered off course due to either a passenger takeover or pilot's change of mind.

8. Plane #2 may have veered off course due to either a passenger takeover or pilot's change of mind.

9. Plane #2 may have hit the same tower as Plane #1 causing only one tower to be destroyed.

10. With the help of standard, built-in anti-hijacking hardware and software, Plane #1 could have been remote-controlled to a safe location or shot down over the ocean.

11. With the help of standard, built-in anti-hijacking hardware and software, Plane #2 could have been remote-controlled to a safe location or shot down over the ocean.

4.3 WTC 1 possible outcomes

The outcomes for WTC 1 include a number of possible outcomes, they are

1. Plane #1 might have flown too low toward WTC 1 and crashed into a different building.

2. Plane #1 might have flown too low toward WTC 1 and only clipped the tower and crashed into a different building.

3. Plane #1 might have flown too low toward WTC 1 and exploded and caused the tower to tip over in an irregular fashion. The fall of the tower could have had extensive damage on the surrounding neighborhood.

4. Plane #1 might have flown into the mid-section of WTC 1 and only clipped the tower causing some destruction to the building but tremendous wing damage that would have led to the plane crashing elsewhere.

5. Plane #1 might have flown into the mid-section of WTC 1, hitting directly but the fuel might not have exploded in the capacity required to collapse the entire tower, especially since the fuel fire would not have reached the upper floors.

6. Plane #1 might have flown toward the mid-section of WTC 1 and missed completely forcing the pilot to spend time and fuel to circle around for another strike.

7. Plane #1 might have flown toward the mid-section of WTC 1 and missed completely but then crashed into a different tower.

8. Plane #1 might have flown toward the top-section of WTC 1 and missed completely but then crashed into a different tower.

9. Plane #1 might have flown toward the top-section of WTC 1 and missed completely forcing the pilot to spend time and fuel to circle around for another strike.

10. Plane #1 might have flown toward the top-section of WTC 1 and only clipped the tower with the wing causing only minor structural damage to the building but damaging the wing of the aircraft and causing the aircraft to crash elsewhere.

11. Plane #1 might have flown toward the top-section of WTC, hit directly, and exploded all of its fuel.

As we continue to itemize the different possible outcomes we get a conservative total of 33 outcomes. Remember that there are two towers (WTC 1 and WTC 2) as targets and two planes (Plane #1 and Plane #2) and two pilots (Pilot #1 and Pilot #2). Once again, I will apply a conservative approach.

In order to get the complete set of outcomes we have to reference each of them. This gives us the total number of potential outcomes. Any combination of these outcomes would produce a significantly different set of events in New York on September 11, 2001. What happened on that day is well known, but what is not well known is what else could have happened. Probability requires us to know the full set of data.

4.4 WTC 2 possible outcomes

The same set of 11 outcomes is true of WTC 2 as it is for WTC 1:

1. Plane #2 might have flown too low toward WTC 2 and crashed into a different building.

2. Plane #2 might have flown too low toward WTC 2 and only clipped the tower and crashed into a different building.

3. Plane #2 might have flown too low toward WTC 2 and exploded and caused the tower to tip over in an irregular fashion. The fall of the tower could have had extensive damage on the surrounding neighborhood.

4. Plane #2 might have flown into the mid-section of WTC 2 and only clipped the tower causing some destruction to the building but tremendous wing damage that would have led to the plane crashing elsewhere.

5. Plane #2 might have flown into the mid-section of WTC 2, hitting directly but the fuel might not have exploded in the capacity required to collapse the entire tower, especially since the fuel fire would not have reached the upper floors.

6. Plane #2 might have flown toward the mid-section of WTC 2 and missed completely forcing the pilot to spend time and fuel to circle around for another strike.

7. Plane #2 might have flown toward the mid-section of WTC 2 and missed completely but then crashed into a different tower.

8. Plane #2 might have flown toward the top-section of WTC 2 and missed completely but then crashed into a different tower.

9. Plane #2 might have flown toward the top-section of WTC 2 and missed completely forcing the pilot to spend time and fuel to circle around for another strike.

10. Plane #2 might have flown toward the top-section of WTC 2 and only clipped the tower with the wing causing only minor structural damage to the building but damaging the wing of the aircraft and causing the aircraft to crash elsewhere.

11. Plane #2 might have flown toward the top-section of WTC, hit directly, and exploded all of its fuel.

4.5 The 3 necessary outcomes

Let's assume that the plane hits high enough. It has to be a direct impact. If it only clipped the tower it wouldn't destroy the tower. And it has to explode all of its fuel. There are many possible outcomes. For example, the plane might strike too low and topple the tower, and the plane might clip the tower and crash. The plane might miss completely and have to circle around more than once to hit its target. Each plane must

1. Hit top-section of tower
2. Have a direct impact
3. Penetrate structure with full fuel explosion

In order to obtain the desired outcomes of two planes each hitting an independent tower and both towers collapsing perfectly into their own footprint, as witnessed by the world and shown in news reports and captured in photographic images, we need to achieve the following outcomes:

5. CHANCE OF HITTING TOWERS

The ideal outcome for both WTC 1 and WTC 2 is Outcome 11. If we have established 33 possible outcomes (conservatively); therefore the chance of hitting the first tower is:

1 in 33

Plane #1 has two possible towers. That means that his chance of achieving the objective is **twice as high** as Plane #2. In probability we have to add these chances together to get the figure.

5.1 The chance to hit calculations

Here's my calculation for Plane #1:

Chance to hit North Tower = 3.0%
(1/33 = 0.0303)

Chance to hit South Tower = 3.0%
(1/33 = 0.0303)

The equation then becomes:

1/33 + 1/33 = 6.1% (0.0303 + 0.0303 = 0.0606)

Plane #1 (flown by Pilot #1) has a 6.1% chance of achieving the desired outcomes: hitting the top-section of the tower, having a direct impact, and penetrating the structure with full fuel explosion.

What are the chances for Plane #2?

Chance of Plane #2 hitting tower = 3.0%
(1/33 = 0.0303)

Plane #2 has no choice but to aim for the undamaged tower, since that is what happened on the day of the event. Plane #2 did not attempt to hit WTC 1.

These aircrafts are full-sized commercial jets flying at 530 mph and weighing in excess of 300,000 pounds. They don't manoeuvre like fighter jets and if they turn too sharp their engines could stall or the planes might flip out of control.

5.2 Probability of hitting two towers

What is the probability of hitting both towers, each one with one of the two hijacked planes?

Using the multiplication rule for a **sequence of events** we get:

$$6.1\% \times 3.0\% = 0.2\% \,(0.00183)$$

The probability of hitting these two towers in the right way is 0.2%. If we work that out to odds we get (roughly):

Odds of hitting both towers is 500 to 1

If we follow the proper probability equation the number is something like 499.99 to 1. For simplicity sake I have rounded the numbers.

In order for all three towers to collapse due to extensive fire and structural damage, as outlined in the 9/11 Commission Report, we need two planes to hit their marks, but their chance of succeeding is only 0.2%. Their chance of failure (roughly) is 99.8%. Let me put it this way, if you wanted to do something crazy and all the experts said that you had a 99% chance of failure, would you still do it? Would you even plan for it or would you plan for something more achievable?

Much to everyone's surprise, and against all odds, each of the two planes over New York perfectly hit their respective targets. Nothing short of a miracle. The damage to the buildings would set off a chain of events that would demoralize the US for no less than 10 years and would lead to the formation of Homeland Security, the installation of airport scanners, new foreign policies, and a prolonged war on foreign soil that would cost in the trillions of dollars.

6. COLLAPSING THE TOWERS

All of the observers, experts, and witnesses stressed the size of the explosion and the fire damage as a result of all the explosive fuel. The presentation of extensive fire and structural damage provided the perfect storm that was believed to have dropped all three towers. Even though Tower 7 was not hit by a plane and had not experienced any fuel fires, the 9/11 investigation identified the fallen debris and the extensive fire damage that weakened the support structures and the integrity of the building such that hours later the third tower was brought down. All of these official explanations defy the long-standing evidence that no steel-structure has ever collapsed without the assistance of professional demolitions.

The conspiracy theorists as well have repeatedly stressed the fact that the temperature from a fuel fire could never reach the melting point of steel and certainly couldn't create molten balls of iron. These alternative, and neglected, experts cite the near free fall collapse of a 1,300-foot structure, the collapse of each tower into its own footprint, and a strange observation that suggests the lack of sufficient debris given the size and height of the towers. Had the towers collapsed due to structural fire damage then there should have been a larger amount of fallen debris. The lack of sufficient debris given the height ratio of the towers supports their hypothesis that high-powered explosives or a cold fusion detonation obliterated some of that debris. Some independent investigators cited the lack of aircraft debris as if the planes themselves evaporated by the fire. Finally, just by careful observation of the points of impact, anyone can clearly see that only a handful of floors on the upper end of the towers were damaged.

Why is all this significant? Because the towers had 110 floors and were over 1,350-feet in height. The North Tower also was fitted with a 360-foot antenna. Each floor was the size of a football field; 40,000 square feet of space. Was there enough burning fuel to spread throughout the entire interior floor space of each tower? How many football fields could the fire consume? The Twin Towers each had nearly 300 steel columns including 50 core columns. In order for a tower to fall, all of the columns would have to fail. Surprisingly, this occurred in all three towers.

When Tower 7's collapse is compared side-by-side with a professionally demolished building, the similarities are uncanny. Both towers drop at near free fall in uniform fashion, yet one building is falling due to fire damage and the other due to demolitions.

For the purpose of our discussion, I will continue to support the fire damage conclusion as presented by the 9/11 Commission and the supplementary NIST and FEMA reports. Two planes struck two towers and three towers fell.

6.1 Odds of collapse due to fire

The probability of each tower collapsing due to fire damage is one-percent (1%).

Odds of the South Tower collapsing = 1%

Odds of South Tower + North Tower collapsing = 1% x 1% = 0.01% (0.0001)

Or

10,000 to 1

Odds of South Tower + North Tower + Tower 7 collapsing:

1% x 1% x 1% = 0.0001% (0.000001)

Or

A million to 1

6.2 A sequence of outcomes

On September 11, 2001, we have this sequence of events. Two planes hit two towers and three towers perfectly collapsed into their own footprint.

Using the multiplication rule for a related sequence of outcomes:

Odds of South Tower + North Tower + Tower 7 Collapsing + 2 Planes Hitting Two Towers:

1% x 1% x 1% x 0.2% = 0.0000002% (0.000000002)

Or

500 million to 1

The odds of all 4 events happening on September 11 are

500 million to 1

The odds of winning the U.S. Powerball lottery are

176 million to 1 (all six numbers)

The odds of winning the lottery in Canada are

15 million to 1

The odds of becoming the president of the United States are only

10 million to 1

A person is more likely to be struck by lightning than to become the US president. And these attackers would have become Presidents of the United States had they attempted that plan instead of targeting office towers in New York with planeloads of people.

6.3   Falling in the footprint

But we're not finished. The three towers didn't just collapse. Actually they collapsed in a very unusual way. All three buildings fell straight down, in nearly free-fall, and into their own footprint. This puzzling and inexplicable evidence convinced the conspiracy theorists that a clandestine group was involved. But the official statements from the experts as well as from the 9/11 Commission Report do not accept the argument that the buildings were destroyed by any other means. No matter they fell uniformly as a result of fire or cold fusion beams, the fact remains that they all fell in a uniform fashion. And that is all we need in order to perform probability analysis. Like I said, for our purposes we don't need to know the grim details. We stick to the facts.

We have already established that the probability of one tower collapsing is one-percent. What is the probability of a tower **collapsing perfectly**? Because I think this is an important distinction. Architects and engineers, when commenting about WTC 7, repeated the argument that in order for a steel-framed building to collapse perfectly into their own footprint it would require controlled demolitions. And since this perfect collapse exists with each of the three towers, it is too anomalous to leave out. But the evidence to prove that demolitions were used is also lacking. All we have is the result and the result is that three towers fell near "free-fall into their own footprint."

Since no official has ever admitted the use of explosives, and will unlikely ever make such a statement, I will continue to rely on the fire argument. But I have one problem to solve—the only time a building collapses in on itself, into its own footprint, is when demolitions are used. That means that in our particular case, not only did the towers collapse, but they collapsed *perfectly*.

"For the buildings to come down as they did, straight down, all 287 steel columns had to fail *simultaneously*. Think about that. And the theory is that it was fire that caused the steel columns to weaken and that's what brought the building down. Well, first of all, steel-framed buildings have never come down due to fire," said theologian David Ray Griffin in an interview with CBC's *The Fifth Estate*.

We have already agreed that the probability of one tower collapsing due to fire is 1%. What then is the probability of a tower collapsing *perfectly*?

Rather than creating a terrifying scenario by choosing larger odds, say 1 in 1,000, since there is no evidence of a steel-framed building ever collapsing perfectly due to fire but we could sum up the total number of steel-framed buildings in the world and use that figure, I think it is more prudent, and fair, that we use Richard Gage's figure from his research of steel-frame building fires: "No steel-framed high rise building has ever collapsed due to fire, and we have over 100 examples from which to choose." He's an architect with over 20 years of practical experience in the field. It is a reliable figure. Of over 100 fires in steel-framed buildings there were no collapses; therefore, on September 11 we have the very first case of this occurrence: hence the 1 in 100 chance. It's not entirely accurate since the odds are much lower but it is entirely fair and illustrates the main point of this argument.

Using the Fire Formula, if we say that for every 100 fire-related collapses one is **perfect** then we have

$$1 \text{ in } 100, \text{ or } 1\%$$

One-percent of steel-framed building collapses from fire will be *perfect*. In our unique case we have three perfect collapses. So now we have to update our figures:

If the probability of each tower **collapsing perfectly** is one-percent then the probability of one tower collapsing is the combination of these two events:

$$1\% \times 1\% = 0.0001$$

Or

10,000:1

It has never happened before. No steel-framed tower has ever collapsed due to fire in the history of earth. Not only that but all three of our towers collapsed perfectly; thereby, introducing the fact that this kind of event is indeed possible. Only that the probability of one tower collapsing in this fashion is very low

10,000 to 1

What is the probability of all three towers (South Tower, North Tower, Tower 7) collapsing perfectly?

Here's the math:

$$.0001 \times .0001 \times .0001 = 0.000000000001$$

Or

One trillion to 1

The odds are **one trillion to one** that three steel structures could collapse due to fire on the same day, as described and observed.

But we're not finished yet. We still have to account for two amateur pilots strategically hitting two of our three towers.

The new math:

$$0.000000000001 \times 0.002 =$$
$$500,000,000,000,000$$

Or

500 trillion to 1

The odds of the sequences of events that perfectly collapsed the three World Trade Center Towers in New York happening on September 11, 2001 are **500 trillion to 1**.

This is a once in a lifetime event. An equivalent event on a grand scale would be an event that never happened before. For example, the Second

Coming of Christ. If Jesus were to manifest himself tomorrow in New York, an event that hasn't occurred for about 2,000 years, why that would match the significance of the 9/11 attacks.

We have this unique sequence of events to explain using math:

(1) Perfect collapse of 3 steel-framed buildings
(2) Two hijacked planes hitting two towers directly
(3) No known outside help

7. CONCLUSION

For the purpose of probability we do not need to know all the details of the September 11 events. We have enough information. All of it well-established and officially sanctioned. Unfortunately, if we were to rely on the fire myth as the reason for all three buildings collapsing perfectly and we believed that the terrorist hijackers were adequately trained in flying a modern Boeing 767 wide-bodied aircraft— an aircraft that is 159 feet long and 156 feet wide weighing about 300,000 pounds and with a cruising speed of 530 mph—if we believe all these things then what has been achieved on that day beat all the odds. The likelihood of these events tells Americans, and observers around the world, that it was a day of magic.

The official 9/11 experts typically talk about the jet fuel fires, the structural damage, and the weakened integrity of the steel-framed buildings as reasons for their perfect collapse, when no steel-framed building has ever collapsed in the history of their making. The fuel-induced collapses would have had to simultaneously remove 287 steel columns. And, generally speaking, fuel fire doesn't even burn hot enough to melt steel let alone the steel in 287 columns hundreds of feet long. Yet people still accept the official explanation.

There is no mistake that the attacks on America on September 11, 2001 did in fact occur. Nearly 3,000 souls were lost on that fateful day. The subsequent invasion of Iraq and Afghanistan, under any number of false premises, took the lives of 4,491 US troops and wounded, injured, or killed hundreds of thousands of people. The US economy has weakened as a result, a debt that will be handed to the next generation.

But the hijacked aircrafts over New York and the collapse of the World Trade Center Towers answers a mathematical mystery that displaces both the official explanation and all of the criminal evidence.

The likelihood of the attacks on New York, specifically, when examined using probability, had a 500 trillion to one chance of occurring.

Two planes crashed into two towers and three towers fell. We've all seen the videos and photographs. We've heard the testimonials. These events happened. Yet according to my conservative math, and I am not a mathematician, the events could not have happened as descried.

There are three probabilities that explain away all the official 9/11 evidence. The first is the probability of two planes each hitting one of the Twin Towers. Without the strikes from the planes there would be no fire to bring down the towers and there'd be no falling debris to knock down WTC 7. **The odds of the planes hitting perfectly are 500 to 1**.

The second probability has to account for **all three towers collapsing due to fire**. Since no steel-framed building has ever collapsed due to fire, this was an unprecedented event and the odds of **one trillion to one** reflect that.

Third, the plane crashes and collapsing towers are all intertwined and therefore become the probability of a sequence of events. All combined, and conservatively speaking, the **odds of the sequences of events taking place in New York are five hundred trillion to one**.

Better than fire

Despite the official 9/11 investigation, the sequence of events in New York simply could not have happened as described. While top experts and eye witnesses were used to explain and inflate the details, and the conspiracy theorists shot down the mainstream ideas, the math did not in any way change. And the events of 9/11 have never seen any new and meaningful investigation. Most Americans accept the official explanation that 19 Islamic hijackers against America committed those heinous acts. Perhaps they need to be informed that the odds of those events happening are impossible, in fact implausible. But since the planes crashed into the towers and all three towers apparently collapsed perfectly into their own footprint, and if the math doesn't lie, then there must be some other factor involved in its success, backing the hijackers.

We cannot deny that these attacks happened. Clearly the three towers in New York fell, impressively so. But my math says that the explanation is wrong. The explanation is fire. It wasn't fire that brought down those buildings because the odds are less than zero. And it wasn't the planes since the planes created the fire, which again is not the reason.

If the fire could not have brought down the towers then the planes no longer have any purpose because the fire excuse won't work. Therefore we can only speculate that there was another key technology, or advanced technique, employed on September 11. Whatever it was may never be known. I doubt the terrorists had any awareness of it.

My math says that some other technology was employed that day and that it was better than fire. Dr. Wood sums it up nicely, "Hot things glow but not everything that glows is hot."

May the new generation have the willpower and insightfulness to finally solve this implausible mystery.

APPENDIX

Boeing 767

Wide-body twin jet airliner, two-crew cockpit

Cruising speed: Mach 0.8 (533 mph/858 km/h) at 35,000 ft (11,000 m)
Maximum speed: Mach 0.86 (587 mph/913 km/h)

Wingspan: 156 ft 1 in (46 m)

Length of plane: 159 ft 2 in (48.5 m)

Weight: 177,000 lb (no cargo, no fuel, no load) to 315,000 lb (max. for takeoff)

Fuel tank: 16,700 US gal (63,000 L)/ 24,100 US gal (ER version)(91,000 L)
Jet fuel weighs 6.8 pounds per gallon. Fuel weight for Flight 175 is 113,500 pounds. Fuel weight for Flight 11 is 163,800 pounds.

Revised weight for Flight 175: 177,000 + 113,500 = 290,500 pounds

Revised weight for Flight 11: 177,000 + 163,800 = 340,800 pounds

Capacity of 181 to 375 persons, range of 3,850 to 6,385 miles (7,130 to 11,825 km)

The 767-200 began service in 1982. The 767-200ER in 1984. The unit cost of the 767-200ER is about $150 million.

Boeing Commercial Airplanes is the manufacturer and has manufactured over 1,000 767s over 30 years.

The World Trade Center

Each of the Twin Towers was 208 feet by 208 feet.

Weight of each tower: 500,000 tons

50,000 people worked in the towers on a daily basis

Ground-breaking for the WTC started on August 5, 1966

Construction on the North Tower began in August 1968 (completed in 1972); the South Tower by January 1969 (completed in 1973).

Tower 1, 1,368 ft (417 m), 110 floors (North) In 1978, a 360 feet (110 m) high telecommunications antenna was added stretching the height of 1 WTC to 1738 feet (527 m).

Tower 2, 1,362 ft (415 m), 110 floors (South)

Each floor had 40,000 square feet of space. Each tower had 3.8 million square feet of office space.

Tower 7, 610 ft (186 m), 47 floors

The World Trade Center was privatized and leased to Silverstein Properties in July 2001.

Paris Tosen